Top 50 Operating System Interview Questions & Answers

Knowledge Powerhouse

DEDICATION

To our readers!

CONTENTS

ACKNOWLEDGMENTS

We thank our readers who constantly send feedback and reviews to motivate us in creating these useful books with the latest information!

INTRODUCTION

Operating System is one of the basic technology topics. There is a growing demand for software engineers in technology companies.

This book contains technical interview questions that an interviewer asks on Operating System subject. Each question is accompanied with an answer so that you can prepare for job interview in short time.

We have compiled this list after attending dozens of technical interviews in top-notch companies like- Uber, IBM, Oracle etc.

Often, these questions and concepts are used in our daily work. But these are most helpful when an Interviewer is trying to test your deep knowledge of Operating System.

Once you go through them in the first pass, mark the questions that you could not answer. Then, in second pass go through only the difficult questions. After going through this book 2-3 times, you will be well prepared to face a technical interview in Operating System area.

Operating System Interview Questions

1. What is the need for an operating system in a computer?

We need an operating system (OS) for following purposes:

- **Manage computer's resources**: OS is responsible for managing all the resources of computer like- cpu, memory, hard drive etc.

- **User interface**: OS provides a user interface to any user working on a computer. The interface provided by OS helps the user to perform a variety of tasks on computer.

- **Service Execution**: OS provides the ability to execute services and programs on a computer. These services can be used by user as well as by other programs on the computer.

2. What is Demand Paging in OS?

Demand Paging is a technique of virtual memory

management in an OS. In case of demand paging, an OS will copy a page from disk into memory only when someone attempts to access this page and the page does not already exist in memory.

The condition in which a page is accessed and it does not exist in memory is called a page fault.

The flow of Demand Paging is as follows:
- A process makes an attempt to access page.
- OS checks if page is in memory.
- If page is in memory it is given to process.
- If page is not in memory, a page fault occurs.
- In case of page fault, there is a mechanism in OS to trap these faults.
- OS checks if the page exists in secondary memory like hard drive.
- If page does not exist in secondary memory, the process is terminated.
- If page exists in secondary memory, the page is read from secondary memory into main memory.
- Once the page brought in main memory, it is given to the interrupted process to do further processing.

3. What are the pros and cons of Demand Paging?

Some of the pros and cons if demand paging are as follows:

Pros:
- It only loads that pages that are required or

demanded by the processes. There is no need to load extra amount of information in memory.

- With demand paging there is more space available in main memory to load more processes. This reduces the amount of context switching.
- Startup of a system is faster with demand paging, because there is no need to load a lot of data in memory.
- Demand paging makes the price of system cheaper, because there is no need to buy expensive memory.

Cons:

- With demand paging, individual programs and processes face delay in accessing the information when they access it the first time.
- Low cost systems may not have support for demand paging.
- Memory management becomes complex with demand paging.

4. What are the main advantages of a system with multiple processors?

A computer system with more than one computing processor unit is called multiprocessor system. These processors can share the memory as well as other peripherals.

The main advantages of multiprocessor system are as follows:

- **Throughput**: The capacity of a system to execute tasks increases with multiple processors. This increases the throughput of the system.

- **Reliability**: The overall reliability of the system increases with the multiple processors. In case, one processor goes down, the system can keep working.
- **Resource sharing**: In a multiple processor system, the resources are shared. This increases the efficiency of resource utilization.
- **Cost**: Initially multiple processor systems cost more, but with the increased efficiency it is cheaper to use multi-processor systems in long run.

5. What is kernel in OS?

Kernel is the core program of an operating system. It is the central program that has control over everything in the computer.

Generally, the Kernel is the first program to be loaded into memory during start-up time of a system.

Kernel handles the input out communication requests, connections to peripherals like keyboard, monitor, and translation of programming instructions into cpu specific language.

Kernel is considered a low level component in OS. A request made to kernel is called system call.

Some of the important functions of kernel are device management, memory management, resource management and system calls.

6. What is a Real time system?

A Real time system is a hardware and software system that works within the constraint of real time. It means, the system has to respond with guarantee within a timeframe to a request.

The examples of Real time system are, flight control system, anti lock brake system in car, time constrained chess playing software.

Due to strict deadlines, Real time system is a mission critical system. It has to make sure that various scenarios of failure do not hamper its performance of responding in real time.

There are three main categories of real time systems.
- Hard real time
- Firm real time
- Soft real time

7. What is Virtual memory in OS?

Virtual memory (VM) is also known as Virtual storage. It is a memory management technique.

In VM, the operating system uses a combination of hardware and software system to make it appear to users that they have a large memory.

OS maps the memory addresses used by program to physical memory addresses. The addresses used by program are called virtual address. The hardware part of address translation in the system is called memory management unit (MMU).

VM provides the benefit of freeing applications from doing any separate memory management. Also VM makes higher amount of memory than the physical memory available to application. VM helps in enhancing the security by isolating the memory.

8. What is multi processing in OS?

Multi-processing in OS is used for executing multiple processes at the same time. This gives better throughput from the system.

Multi-processing appears similar to multi-tasking. In multitasking, same CPU is used for running multiple processes. In multi-processing more than one processor is used for executing multiple processes.

Multi-processing leads to higher CPU utilization and better user experience.

9. What is a Time sharing system?

A Time sharing system is also known as multi tasking system. In a time sharing system, same CPU is used for running multiple programs.

One of the popular ways of multi-tasking, is round robin approach. In this approach, each process is given turn to execute in a sequential round robin order.

The other way of multi-tasking is time slicing. In this

scheme, CPU time is shared between multiple processed.

10. What is a Thread in OS?

In OS, a Thread of execution is the smallest unit of instructions that can be managed by a scheduler.

A Thread is also considered as a component of a process.

Thread comprises of an ID, program counter, register set and stack.

Thread contains less state information than a process. Threads of a process often share the address space.

Context switching between threads is much faster than the context switching between processes.

11. What are the advantages of multi-threaded programming?

The main advantages of multi-threaded programming are as follows:

- **User response**: Multi-thread programming provides enhanced response to a user.
- **Economical**: It is less costly to run a multi-threaded system. The multi-threaded programming provides high throughput for the less amount of investment.
- **Resource sharing**: Multi-threaded programming helps in sharing of resources among processed.
- **Efficient**: Multi-threading leads to better utilization of the overall system.

12. What is FCFS in OS?

FCFS stands for first come first served. It is used as a scheduling algorithm in OS. In FCFS, the process that requests for CPU first, is given the first priority of execution.

It is similar to a queue mechanism in real life. People exit the queue in the order of their arrival.

Similarly in FCFS, a queue is used to maintain the order of processes. The scheduler uses this queue to find the next process eligible for execution.

13. What is Round Robin scheduling algorithm in OS?

In Round Robin (RR) algorithm, the scheduler assigns a fixed time unit to each process. If the process is able to execute its instructions within this time unit, then it exits and the remaining time is given to the next process. If the process is not able to finish its execution in this time unit, it gets rescheduled and another process if given the CPU time.

RR uses a circular queue to maintain the order of processes.

The benefit of RR is that it avoids starvation of a process. Even a process with lower priority gets some CPU time in RR scheduling algorithm.

14. What is a Deadlock in OS?

In an OS, deadlock happens, when a process goes to waiting state for a resource that is already held by another process in waiting state. Due to this both the processes keep waiting for each other's resource.

Deadlock can also occur between more than two processes when each process is waiting for the resource held by another process in a circular way.

15. What are the necessary conditions for Deadlock to occur?

The necessary conditions for a Deadlock are as follows:
- **Mutual exclusion**: In deadlock, at least one resource should be held in non-shareable mode. It means, only one process can use that resource at a time.
- **Hold and wait**: In deadlock, the process should be in waiting state for a resource held by another process.
- **No pre-emption**: For a deadlock to occur, the resource can be released only voluntarily by a process. The OS can not preempt the resource from the process holding it.
- **Circular wait:** In a deadlock situation, there is a circular wait for resources among the processes in deadlock.

16. What is Banker's algorithm in

OS?

The Banker's algorithm is a deadlock avoidance algorithm in OS. It was developed by Edsger Dijkstra.

It is based on the algorithm in banking system where a bank never runs out of cash because bank does not allocate money in such a way that it can not satisfy the needs of a customer.

Banker's algorithm takes three things into consideration:
What is the max amount of each resource each process can request.
What is the amount of each resource being held by each process.
What is the amount of each resource currently available in system.

With the help of this data, Banker's algorithm finds if the system can get into a deadlock or not. If a request is safe, it is granted permission. If a request makes the system unsafe, it will be denied.

17. What is the difference between logical and physical address space?

The physical address space refers to actual physical address in the memory unit. Where as, logical address space is the list of addresses generated by CPU. Logical address space is also known as virtual address.

In an OS, memory management unit (MMU) is responsible for mapping the logical address to physical address. With the help of MMU, memory management techniques like demand paging etc can be implemented in OS.

18. What is the use of dynamic loading in memory management?

With Dynamic loading, a computer program can load a library at run time. Once a library is loaded, the instructions in the library can be executed in memory. It is a popular way of one program using another program.

Dynamic loading allows a computer program to start in absence of the required libraries in memory. As an when the need arises, the libraries are loaded in memory. Since the amount of memory is limited in a system, the dynamic loading allows for better memory management by loading only required libraries in memory.

19. What is an overlay in OS?

The overlay is a programming technique by which the program is allowed to be larger than the main memory of a computer system. Overlay is used in OS for embedded system because physical memory is scarce in an embedded system.

In an overlay system, the program is divided into self-contained object code blocks called overlays that are stored in a tree like structure. An overlay manager is responsible for loading the required overlay from external memory into the destination region.

From 2015 onwards, most of the computer system use virtual memory. This has reduced the popularity of overlay.

20. What is fragmentation?

Fragmentation is a phenomenon in storage space management. When storage space is used inefficiently, it leads to fragmentation. There is wastage of storage space in fragmentation.

There are three types of fragmentation: External fragmentation, Internal fragmentation, and Data fragmentation.

In a computer system, blocks of memory are allocated in chunks. Once the use of memory is done, program releases the chunks. When computer starts, the free memory space is allocated in contiguous manner. But later, with allocation and freeing up of memory blocks in a random manner, the free memory space becomes fragmented.

Due to fragmentation, many problems like storage failure, performance degradation etc can occur.

One of the popular option to reduce fragmentation is defragmentation. It is a process to reduce the fragmentation by organizing disk space in contiguous blocks.

21. What are the different states of a process in system?

In a system, a process can be in one of the following

states:
- New: In this state, the process is created.
- Ready/Waiting: This is the state in which a process is loaded into memory, but it is waiting to be executed by CPU.
- Running: This is the state in which the instructions of process are getting executed by cpu.
- Blocked: In this state, the process is can not carry on executing because some external condition has to occur. Eg. A process may be blocked on a call to an input output device like printer.
- Terminated: A process may be put in terminated state from running state or it may be killed forcibly.
- Swapped out and waiting: In this state, the process is removed from the main memory. But it is waiting to be swapped back into main memory for further execution.
- Swapped out and blocked: In this state, the process is blocked and it is removed from the main memory.

22. What is a socket in OS?

A socket is a mechanism of inter process communication. It is a data communications endpoint. Two processed can exchange data between them by using a common socket. Socket supports ordered/unordered and reliable exchange of information between two processes.
TCP socket and UDP socket are popular examples of socket in unix systems.

In Unix, sockets use file system as their address name

space. Generally a socket is identified by an address (IP address) and a port on a system.

Some of the popular system calls on a socket are getSocket(), connect(), send() and close().

23. What is Thrashing in OS?

Thrashing is a condition in a system, when virtual memory resources become saturated and system goes into constant state of paging. Paging is the state in which there is rapid exchange of data between memory and disk.

The performance of a system degrades with thrashing. The symptom of thrashing is high page fault rate.

CPU is so much busy in handling high page fault rate, that it can not handle user requests. This leads to user getting slow system performance.

Some of the types of thrashing are: Cache thrashing, Translation look aside buffer (TLB) thrashing, heap thrashing, process thrashing.

24. What is a boot partition in OS?

Boot partition in OS is also referred as system partition. A boot partition is a disk partition that must exist and configured correctly for a computer to operate.

The boot partition contains the boot loader. This is the software responsible for booting the operating system.

The system partition is the disk partition that contains the operating system folder.

In certain systems, boot and system partition can be located in same disk partition.

25. What is a device driver?

A device driver is a computer program that is used for controlling and operating a device attached to the computer. It is like a software interface between hardware device and operating system.

The device driver communicates with the device by using the computer bus. Device driver is responsible for issuing commands to the device.

In general, device driver is a hardware dependent software. It is also specific to an operating system.

When we connect same printer to another operating system, it may need a different device driver.

26. What are the pros and cons of command line interface (CLI) in an OS?

A command line interface (CLI) provides an interface to a user to give commands to a computer system. CLI executes the commands and sends the result back to user.

CLI is very useful for interacting with system. Users with expert knowledge can effectively tune and run processes on system by using CLI. For manual work, expert user can type commands very fast and they can get their work done very fast on a computer.

The issue with CLI is that it needs specialized knowledge of commands. It requires memorization of commands by user. Where as, in a menu based user interface like Windows, there is no need to remember the commands. User can explore the commands whenever it is necessary.

27. What is spooling?

Spooling is a kind of multi-programming. It is often used in the context of printer.

In modern systems, the computer hands off the printing task to printer and proceeds with the other tasks. The printer keeps doing the work at its own pace.

There is a spooler program in the system that maintains the sequence and order of tasks. It keeps sending tasks to printer in the order specified to it.

Spooling can also be considered as a hybrid approach that makes used of buffering and queuing.

28. What is an assembler?

An assembler is a computer program. It performs translation of assembly codes into machine language.

Assembler is a low level program. It understands the assembly language instructions. It converts these instructions into binary 0 1 representation understood by computer hardware.

29. What is an Interrupt?

An interrupt is a system programming concept. The interrupt is a signal sent to the processor by a hardware or software.

The interrupt occurs in response to an event that needs immediate attention. By using an interrupt, we can alert the processor to take a high priority event into consideration.

Pressing a key on keyboard or mouse movement are the examples of hardware interrupt.

A divide by zero condition in a program is the example of a software interrupt.

Every interrupt has to be handled by a specific interrupt handler.

We can also use an interrupt to kill a process in system.

30. What is pre-emptive multitasking in OS?

Pre-emptive multitasking refers to the technique used by computers to provide fair chance to each process for execution in a multi-tasking environment.

In preemptive multitasking, OS assigns a fixed slice of operating time to every process. In case a process is not able to finish its task within this time period, it is taken out of execution. Later when its turn comes again, the context switch is done by OS to give operating time to this process.

Basic concept behind preemptive multitasking is the ability

of OS to preempt a process from execution and bring it back when there is time slice available.

31. Why do we have to partition and format disk before installing an OS?

We need to partition a disk to create space on disk on which operating system can be copied and installed. This is also known as primary partition or system partition.

The file system can lie on another partition. If the partition containing the file system gets corrupt, it does not affect the primary partition on which operating system is installed.

We have to format the drive to prepare it for partitioning. By formatting a drive, we make it ready for initial use. Once a disk is formatted, we can perform partitioning on it.

32. What are the differences between a process and thread?

A thread is also considered as a light weight process. Thread has properties similar to a process.

Some of the differences between a thread and a process are as follows:

A process is a completely independent entity, where as a thread is a subset of a process.

A process contains more state information than a thread. Multiple threads share the same state information.

A process has separate address space. A thread may share the address space with other threads.

A process uses the system provided inter process communication methods. A thread has more methods of communication.

The context switching between processes is much slower than the context switching between threads.

33. What are the different strategies of handling deadlocks in OS?

An OS can use following strategies to handle deadlocks.

- **Ignore**: An OS can ignore the Deadlock condition. It is useful when the time interval between deadlocks is very large and data loss is minimum.

- **Prevention**: An OS can follow strategies to prevent the deadlock from occurring. One popular way of prevention is removal of mutual exclusion condition of deadlock.

- **Detection**: An OS can also detect a deadlock after it occurs, and then take action to come out of deadlock. It can terminate the process causing the deadlock or it can preempt the resource on which deadlock has occurred.

34. What are the different kinds of file systems?

Some of main kinds of file systems are as follows:
- Disk file system
- Flash file system
- Tape file system
- Database file system
- Transactional file system
- Network file system
- Device file system

35. What is a file system?

In an operating system, file system is the program that controls how the data is stored and retrieved. If we do not have a filesystem, then the information will be stored in one very big block. Therefore, it is useful to divide the information in small chunks and then store it.

A filesystem, divides the information into chunks and gives a name/id to each chunk. These small chunks of information are called files.

The file system manages the structure of storing files and the rules of accessing data from files.

Generally filesystem implementation varies with the underlying hardware used for storing the data.

36. What are the important

aspects to consider while designing a file system?

Some the important aspects to consider while designing the file system are as follows:

- Space management
- File naming scheme
- Directory naming
- File Metadata
- File utilities
- Access control to files
- Integrity of data
- User interaction

37. What is Cache in computer system?

A cache in computer system is a hardware or software component to provide fast access to data stored in it.

When a program makes a request for data, if the data exists in cache, it is considered as cache hit. If the data does not exist in cache, it is considered as cache miss.

Cache is generally a costly component in system. Therefore data stored in a cache has to carefully selected.

The use of cache improves the throughput of system.

Caching enhances the bandwidth as well as latency of the system.

Some of the examples of hardware cache are: CPU cache,

GPU cache, DSPs etc.

Some of the examples of software cache are: Disk cache, Web cache etc.

38. What is Memoization?

Memoization is a technique to speed up the execution of computer programs by storing the results of expensive or intermediate function calls in a cache. It is an optimization strategy.

E.g. If we have to write a program to calculate the factorial of N, then we can use following formula.
$f(N) = f(N-1) * N$

In this case we can keep storing the f(N-1), f(N-2) etc values in cache, so that there is no need to calculate these values multiple times.

39. What is a distributed operating system?

A distributed operating system is used to manage a group of computers spread across multiple locations. From distributed operating system's perspective, it appears as if it is a single computer.

With the enhancements in networking, it is possible to run a single task on multiple computers. In this case, distributed operating system makes it appear as if it is running on one computer.

40. How does an Operating System provide security?

An OS controls the access to important resources in the computer system to make it secure.

OS has to distinguish between the requests that are from authenticated users and the requests that are from unauthenticated users. OS rejects the unauthorized access requests to keep the system secure.

OS performs authentication and authorization of users and programs to make sure that only authorized users and programs are able to access the system.

41. What is a virtual machine?

A virtual machine (VM) is an emulation of computer system. A VM provides the functionality of a physical computer.

We can run more than one VM on same hardware system. It means we can get the functionality of multiple computers on same physical hardware.

A VM provides the mechanism to run different kinds of OS on same hardware. We can run Windows and Linux VM on same computer.

The VM running on a system is referred as a guest system. The underlying hardware system is referred as host.

Some of the popular types of VM are: System Virtual Machine and Process Virtual Machine.

One of the good example of process VM is Java Virtual

Machine (JVM).

42. What are the various mechanisms of inter process communication in OS?

Some of the popular mechanisms of inter process communication in OS are as follows:

- File
- Signal/Interrupt
- Socket
- Message Queue
- Pipe
- Shared memory
- Message passing

43. What is process synchronization in OS?

Process synchronization in OS refers to the mechanism that ensures that two or more processes do not execute a program in critical section.

With process synchronization, when one thread starts executing the critical section, the other thread waits for it to complete.

Process synchronization is very important in avoiding race condition between processes.

Process synchronization also helps in dealing with deadlock, starvation, priority inversion and busy waiting.

44. What is busy waiting in OS?

Busy waiting refers to the condition in OS when a process is frequently checking if a condition is true or not. E.g. A program checking when a keyboard input is available.

Busy waiting is also known as Busy looping or spinning.

Busy waiting is sometimes necessary in a controlled manner. Sometimes, Busy waiting can cause decrease in throughput due to do-nothing cycles on CPU.

Busy waiting is considered as an anti-pattern and it should be avoided to utilize the processor efficiently.

45. Why is Unix considered as a secure OS?

Unix has implemented some of the best security techniques to make the OS secure. These techniques are:

Permissions: There is a permissions system in Unix that is used to set different kinds of access to a file or resource in Unix.
User groups: Unix has a user group management system. This user group system can be used to assign permissions and access to users as well as groups.
Root access: In Unix, there is a root user that has access to everything in the system. As long as root user is not compromised, an administrator can take control of the system. Root programmed is not used for day to day purposes. This makes it a secure account.
Passwords: In Unix, we can set strong passwords to keep the user accounts secure.

SUDO: In Unix, root access is not used for every day purpose. There is a convenient sudo command that can be used to switch user to enhanced access.

46. What is the difference between mutex and semaphore in OS?

Mutex as well as semaphore are kernel resources in OS. We use mutex as well as semaphore for process synchronization.

A Mutex is a mutually exclusive locking mechanism. A mutex allows only one process to access the resource at a time. Either a producer or consumer can have to key to mutex and do work. As long as the buffer is used by producer, the consumer has to wait.

A Semaphore is a generalized form of mutex. It is like a signaling mechanism. In a semaphore, once the task is done, a process can signal to other processes that the resource is released and other processes are eligible to access that resource. OS can assign resource to a process as per the priority mechanism.

We can even use Semaphore to track the multiple copies of a resource. Once all the copies are in use, no other process can access the resource. As soon as a copy of the resource is available, the semaphore can be used to signal all the processes waiting for that resource.

47. What is Network Operating System (NOS)?

A Network Operating System (NOS) can be used for two distinct purposes.
a. An operating system for a networking device like router, switch etc.
b. An operating system for managing resources over a network.

NOS can be used to handle multiple kinds of networking scenarios like peer to peer, client server etc.

In a peer to peer system all the computers are considered as equal. In a client server system, one system acts as a server and other systems act as client to server. Client sends the request and server handles it.

48. What is Graphic User Interface (GUI) in OS?

Traditionally OS was considered as a back end system that was handled by experts. With the rise of personal computing, there was a need for an interface through which users can perform tasks on a computer. A GUI provides this interface to users, through which they can access the programs of computer and run their tasks.

A GUI makes it easier to interact with the computer system. An OS like Windows, MacOS provides the GUI functionality to user. The OS handles all the underlying communication that happens through various system peripherals like keyboard and mouse and provides input output to user though GUI.

The alternative to GUI is command line interface (CLI). CLI is considered as useful by people with specialized knowledge.

49. What is Docker?

Docker is a program that provides operating system level virtualization. It is also called containerization.

We can use Docker to run containers. A container is a software package.

A container can be used to run a client server system, a database server, a web server etc.

Containers are very light weight. These are run by a single operating system kernel.

In Docker, containers are created from images that specify the content of a container.

Docker is very popular on Linux platform. Docker makes use of Linux kernel to provide lightweight environment to containers.

50. What is an inode?

An inode is a data structure in Unix file system. It is used to describe a file or directory in filesystem. We can store attributes, disk location etc in an inode.

Attributes like time of last change, access change, owner, permissions etc can be stored in an inode.

We can run ls -i command to get inode number of a file.

Internally there is a table of inodes stored in OS. It is used for finding inode contents and file location during file operations.

What Next?

We hope you have enjoyed the book and learnt Operating System interview questions. To complete your preparation, you might want to read our book on **Microservices Interview Questions**.

We have a video course on Udemy.com with latest questions on Microservices Technical Interview.

Enjoy our promotional coupon **KPOWER10** to get it for just $10 for a limited time.

Once you buy, the course is available for lifetime access.

Course: Microservices Interview Questions Preparation

Link: https://www.udemy.com/microservices-interview-questions/?couponCode=KPOWER10

Want to go higher in your career?

Take your career to the next level with these knowledgeable books on the latest technology areas.

- Top 50 Amazon AWS Interview Questions

- Microservices Interview Questions

- Top 50 Cloud Computing Interview Questions

- Top 100 Spring Interview Questions

- Top 100 GIT Interview Questions

- Top 50 Java 8 Latest Interview Questions

- Top 50 Unix Interview Questions

- Top 50 Java Design Pattern Interview Questions

- Top 100 Java Tricky Interview Questions

- Top 50 SQL Tricky Interview Questions

- Top 50 Hibernate Interview Questions

- Top 200 Java Technical Interview Questions

- Top 100 Java Collections Interview Questions

- Top 100 Java Multi-threading Interview Questions

THANKS

If you enjoyed this book in any way, then I'd like to ask you for a favor. Would you be kind enough to leave a review for this book on Amazon.com?

Link: https://www.amazon.com/Knowledge-Powerhouse/e/B01N5XFZQQ/ref=dp_byline_cont_ebooks_1

It'd be greatly appreciated!

REFERENCES

https://www.linux.org/

http://www.opengroup.org/unix

www.ingramcontent.com/pod-product-compliance
Lightning Source LLC
LaVergne TN
LVHW092029060326
832903LV00059B/736